CHAT GPT FOR BEGINNERS

The introductory guide to fully utilize the potential of Artificial Intelligence-based text generation system to monetize and improve professional and personal life

RYAN WESTWOOD

© **Copyright 2023 - All rights reserved.**

The content contained within this book may not be reproduced, duplicated or transmitted without direct written permission from the author or the publisher.

Under no circumstances will any blame or legal responsibility be held against the publisher, or author, for any damages, reparation, or monetary loss due to the information contained within this book. Either directly or indirectly. You are responsible for your own choices, actions, and results.

Legal Notice:

This book is copyright protected. This book is only for personal use. You cannot amend, distribute, sell, use, quote or paraphrase any part, or the content within this book, without the consent of the author or publisher.

Disclaimer Notice:

Please note the information contained within this document is for educational and entertainment purposes only. All effort has been executed to present accurate, up to date, and reliable, complete information. No warranties of any kind are declared or implied. Readers acknowledge that the author is not engaging in the rendering of legal, financial, medical or professional advice. The content within this book has been derived from various sources. Please consult a licensed professional before attempting any techniques outlined in this book.

By reading this document, the reader agrees that under no circumstances is the author responsible for any losses, direct or indirect, which are incurred as a result of the use of the information contained within this document, including, but not limited to, — errors, omissions, or inaccuracies.

Introduction

Welcome to Chat GPT for Beginners, the introductory guide to fully utilise the potential of Artificial Intelligence-based text generation system to monetise and improve professional and personal life. In today's fast-paced world, we are constantly seeking innovative solutions to simplify our lives and work more efficiently. GPT (Generative Pre-training Transformer) Chat is one such technological innovation that has taken the world by storm.

GPT Chat is an AI-based text generation system that has the ability to generate human-like responses to user inputs. It is designed to understand and respond to natural language inputs, making it an ideal tool for various industries and fields, such as customer service, sales, marketing, education, healthcare, and more. With GPT Chat, you can automate routine tasks, provide personalised customer experiences, and generate engaging content, among other benefits.

In this book, we will provide you with a comprehensive introduction to GPT Chat and how it works. We will explore the history and development of GPT Chat, its applications, advantages, and disadvantages, as well as the differences between GPT Chat versions, including the highly anticipated GPT-4. We will also discuss best practices for designing and implementing GPT Chat systems, as well as case studies and examples of successful GPT Chat implementations.

Introduction

Whether you are a business owner, a marketer, a customer service representative, or simply someone interested in exploring the potential of GPT Chat, this book is for you. We hope to provide you with the knowledge and tools necessary to fully utilise the potential of GPT Chat and improve your personal and professional life.

Thank you for choosing Chat GPT for Beginners as your introductory guide to the world of GPT Chat. Let's get started!

1

Definition and Overview of GPT Chat

GPT Chat (Generative Pre-training Transformer Chat) is an AI-based text generation system that is designed to understand and respond to natural language inputs in a conversational manner. It is a type of chatbot that utilises deep learning algorithms and natural language processing to generate human-like responses to user inputs.

GPT Chat was developed by OpenAI, a research organisation dedicated to advancing AI in a safe and beneficial manner. GPT Chat is based on a neural network architecture called the transformer, which allows it to generate responses that are contextually relevant and grammatically correct.

GPT Chat has been trained on vast amounts of text data, including books, articles, and websites, making it capable of generating responses on a wide range of topics. It has been designed to provide personalised experiences to users, whether it be for customer service, sales, marketing, or other purposes.

One of the key advantages of GPT Chat is its ability to continuously learn from user interactions, allowing it to improve over time and provide better responses to users. It can also handle multiple inputs and generate responses that are contextually relevant to each input.

GPT Chat has numerous applications in various industries and fields, including customer service and support, sales and marketing, education and training, healthcare and medicine, and more. With its ability to automate routine tasks, provide personalised experiences, and generate engaging content, GPT Chat has the potential to revolutionise the way we communicate and interact with technology.

In summary, GPT Chat is an AI-based text generation system that utilises deep learning algorithms and natural language processing to generate human-like responses to user inputs in a conversational manner. It has numerous applications in various industries and fields and has the potential to revolutionise the way we communicate with technology.

2

Historical Development of GPT Chat

The development of GPT Chat can be traced back to the early days of artificial intelligence and natural language processing research in the 1950s and 1960s. Researchers began exploring the potential of machine learning algorithms and natural language processing to create chatbots that could simulate human-like conversation.

However, it wasn't until the 2010s that significant advancements were made in chatbot technology. In 2011, Apple introduced Siri, a voice-activated personal assistant that could respond to natural language inputs. This was followed by the introduction of Google Assistant and Amazon Alexa, which utilised machine learning algorithms to provide personalised experiences to users.

In 2015, researchers introduced the concept of transformers, a neural network architecture that was specifically designed for natural language processing. This architecture allowed for significant improvements in the quality of language models, leading to the development of more sophisticated chatbots.

In 2018, OpenAI introduced the first version of GPT (Generative Pre-training Transformer), a language model that was trained on vast amounts of text data and was capable of generating human-like responses to text inputs. GPT was a significant breakthrough in natural language processing and chatbot technology, and it quickly gained popularity among developers and researchers.

The success of GPT prompted the development of subsequent versions, including GPT-2 and GPT-3. GPT-2, which was released in 2019, was a significant improvement over the original version, with the ability to generate coherent and contextually relevant text on a wide range of topics. However, due to concerns about the potential misuse of the technology, OpenAI chose not to release the full model and only made smaller versions available to the public.

GPT-3, which was released in 2020, was a major breakthrough in natural language processing and chatbot technology. With 175 billion parameters, it was the largest and most powerful language model ever created, capable of generating human-like responses that were almost indistinguishable from those written by humans. GPT-3 also introduced the concept of zero-shot learning, allowing it to generate responses to prompts it had never seen before.

As of the writing of this book, OpenAI is working on the development of GPT-4, which is expected to be even more powerful and capable than its predecessor. While the exact release date of GPT-4 is unknown, it is clear that the development of GPT Chat and natural language processing technology will continue to evolve and revolutionise the way we communicate with technology.

3

What does model language look like?

Model language refers to the use of language that is considered to be of high quality, effective, and impactful. It is often used as a benchmark or standard for others to follow in their own writing and communication.

Model language can take many forms, depending on the context and purpose of the communication. In general, it is characterised by clarity, conciseness, and precision. It avoids ambiguity and uses strong, active verbs to convey meaning.

In written communication, model language often features proper grammar, punctuation, and spelling. It uses sentence structure that is varied and interesting, and it avoids repetition and unnecessary jargon or technical terms. The use of appropriate transitions and cohesive devices enhances the flow of the message. It may also include rhetorical devices such as metaphors, analogies, and similes to help convey meaning in a more engaging and memorable way.

In oral communication, model language is characterised by clear enunciation, appropriate volume, and effective use of tone and inflection. It is well-paced, avoiding too much haste or too much hesitation, and it uses appropriate gestures and body language to reinforce the message.

Model language is essential for effective communication in a variety of professional settings. In business, for example, it can be used in emails, reports, and presentations to convey complex ideas and persuade others. In academia, model language is critical for communicating research findings and scholarly ideas in a clear and concise manner. In journalism, model language can be used to write engaging articles that capture readers' attention.

Ultimately, model language is language that achieves its intended purpose effectively and efficiently. It communicates ideas and information clearly and memorably, leaving a positive impression on the audience. By striving to use model language in our own communication, we can improve our effectiveness as communicators and achieve our desired outcomes.

4

How GPT Chat Works

GPT Chat, also known as a GPT-based chatbot, works by using a pre-trained neural network model to generate responses to user inputs. The neural network model used in GPT Chat is based on the transformer architecture, which was specifically designed for natural language processing tasks.

The training process for GPT Chat involves feeding the neural network model with large amounts of text data, such as books, articles, and web pages. This allows the model to learn the patterns and relationships between words and sentences, and to build a comprehensive understanding of the language it is trained on.

Once the model has been trained, it can be used to generate responses to user inputs. When a user inputs a text message or question, the model analyses the input and generates a response that is intended to be contextually relevant and human-like. The generated response is based on the patterns and relationships the model has learned during the training process.

One of the key features of GPT Chat is its ability to generate responses that are not limited to a specific set of predefined answers or commands. Instead, GPT Chat can generate responses that are contextually relevant to the user's input, regardless of the specific wording or phrasing used.

To achieve this level of flexibility, GPT Chat uses a technique called "prompt engineering," which involves providing the model with specific prompts or instructions on how to generate responses to different types of inputs. These prompts help guide the model's response generation process, allowing it to produce relevant and coherent responses.

GPT (Generative Pre-trained Transformer) chat is a type of artificial intelligence (AI) that is designed to simulate human-like conversation. It is built using deep learning techniques that allow it to learn from massive amounts of text data, enabling it to generate responses to user prompts in natural language.

GPT chat works by using complex algorithms that analyse the input provided by the user and generate a response based on its understanding of language. The system uses a neural network that can learn patterns in language, which enables it to produce coherent and contextually appropriate responses to a wide range of queries.

One of the key benefits of GPT chat is that it can help to streamline communication between humans and machines. For example, businesses can use GPT chat to automate customer service, allowing customers to receive quick and accurate responses to their queries, without the need for human intervention.

GPT chat also has applications in education and training, where it can be used to provide personalised learning experiences for students. It can generate quizzes, provide feedback, and answer questions in real-time, helping students to learn at their own pace and receive immediate support when they need it.

As the technology behind GPT chat continues to advance, it has the potential to revolutionise the way we communicate with machines, making interactions more natural and intuitive. However, it is important to note that GPT chat is not without limitations. The technology is still developing, and there are concerns around the potential for biases in the language and data used to train the models. Nonetheless, GPT chat remains an exciting area of AI research with promising applications across a wide range of industries and fields.

GPT Chat works by using a pre-trained neural network model that has learned the patterns and relationships between words and sentences in a given language. This model is used to generate contextually relevant and human-like responses to user inputs, using prompts and instructions to guide the response generation process.

5

Advantages and disadvantages of GPT Chat

GPT Chat, like any technology, has its strengths and weaknesses, and it's essential to understand them to fully harness its potential.

One of the most significant advantages of GPT Chat is its efficiency. It can generate responses quickly and accurately, reducing response times and improving user satisfaction. It's also highly scalable, allowing businesses to handle a large volume of inquiries with minimal resources.

GPT Chat's ability to provide 24/7 support is another significant advantage. It can handle inquiries at any time of day, making it an ideal solution for businesses with a global customer base or those with limited resources for customer support.

Moreover, GPT Chat's ability to personalise interactions with users is a game-changer. By collecting and analysing data on user behaviour and preferences, it can provide more targeted and customised responses, improving user satisfaction and loyalty.

However, there are also limitations to consider. GPT Chat lacks emotional intelligence, which can impact the user experience when dealing with emotional messages. While it can generate accurate responses based on data, it may struggle to provide empathetic or nuanced responses, which can lead to user frustration.

Additionally, GPT Chat's effectiveness is highly dependent on the quality and quantity of training data. Biased, incomplete, or inaccurate training data can result in biased, incomplete, or inaccurate responses, highlighting the importance of high-quality training data.

GPT Chat may also struggle with open-ended questions and maintaining context in multi-turn conversations, which can limit its effectiveness in certain use cases. It's also limited in its proficiency in different languages, which can impact its ability to serve a diverse user base.

Lastly, there are ethical considerations to keep in mind when using GPT Chat. It has the potential for misuse, such as generating fake news or propaganda. Responsible use of the technology is crucial to mitigate these risks.

By understanding the advantages and disadvantages of GPT Chat and addressing its limitations, we can fully utilise its potential and provide better user experiences.

6

Limitations of GPT Chat

As exciting as the potential of GPT Chat may be, it's important to recognise its limitations. Like any technology, GPT Chat has its strengths and weaknesses that impact its effectiveness in different use cases.

One of the most significant limitations of GPT Chat is its lack of common sense reasoning. While it can generate responses based on patterns it has learned from training data, it doesn't have the ability to apply common sense reasoning or contextual knowledge. This can result in responses that don't fully address the user's needs or questions.

Another limitation is its dependence on training data. The quality and quantity of the training data used to train GPT Chat has a direct impact on its effectiveness. Biased, incomplete, or inaccurate training data can result in biased, incomplete, or inaccurate responses from the chatbot.

GPT Chat also struggles with open-ended questions and maintaining context in multi-turn conversations. It may not have the ability to provide relevant responses to more complex or varied questions, or keep track of context over multiple turns in a conversation.

Furthermore, GPT Chat lacks emotional intelligence and may struggle to provide appropriate responses to emotional messages or provide meaningful advice or insights on certain topics. It's also limited in its proficiency in different languages, which may impact its effectiveness in serving a diverse user base.

Perhaps the most significant limitation of GPT Chat is its potential for misuse. It can be used to generate fake news, propaganda, or other types of malicious content, highlighting the importance of ethical considerations and responsible use of the technology.

As we continue to explore the potential of GPT Chat, it's important to understand and address these limitations to ensure that we use the technology effectively and responsibly.

7

How to create GPT Chat account

To get started with the ChatGPT model on OpenAI's website (https://openai.com/), follow these steps:

1 Look for the "Sign Up" button located at the top right corner of the homepage and click it.

2 Provide your personal details, such as your name, email address, and preferred password.

3 Click the "Create Account" button.

4 Check your email inbox for a verification link, and click it to activate your account.

5 Sign in to your account using your email and password.

6 Navigate to the "Developers" section and select the "Create API Key" button.

7 Choose a name for your API key and click "Create."

8 Your API key will appear on the screen and can also be found in the "API Keys" section of your account.

9 Use this API key to access the ChatGPT model and begin building your application.

Note that if you plan to use ChatGPT for commercial purposes, you will need to apply for a commercial license through OpenAI's website.

. . .

TRAIN your chatbot

Once your account is set up, it's time to train your chatbot. This involves providing it with training data, which can be in the form of conversations, FAQs, or other relevant documents. The training data helps your chatbot learn how to respond to user inquiries and improve its accuracy over time.

Test your chatbot

After training your chatbot, it's essential to test it to ensure it's working correctly. Testing involves simulating user interactions with your chatbot to identify any issues or areas for improvement. You can use testing tools provided by your platform or third-party testing tools to help streamline the process.

Launch your chatbot

After testing your chatbot, it's time to launch it. This involves integrating it with your website or other platforms, such as messaging apps or social media. Your platform should provide guidance on how to integrate your chatbot, and you may need to work with a developer to complete the integration.

As u can see creating a GPT Chat account is a simple process that involves selecting a platform, signing up for an account, configuring your settings, training your chatbot, testing it, and finally launching it. With the right platform and training, you can create a powerful chatbot that improves your customer experience and streamlines your operations.

8

Neural Networks and Deep Learning

Neural networks and deep learning are a key part of GPT Chat's artificial intelligence technology, and they are widely used in many other fields as well. Neural networks are a type of machine learning algorithm that is modeled after the structure and function of the human brain. They are capable of learning from large datasets, identifying patterns, and making decisions based on that information. Neural networks can be used for many different applications, including image and speech recognition, natural language processing, and even game playing.

Deep learning is a subset of machine learning that is particularly effective at processing unstructured data, such as natural language text. It involves training neural networks on large datasets to identify patterns and relationships within the data. Deep learning algorithms are particularly useful for generating high-quality outputs, such as images or text, that are difficult to produce with traditional programming techniques.

In the context of GPT Chat, neural networks and deep learning are used to generate human-like responses to user input. The system is trained on large amounts of text data, which allows it to learn how to generate text that mimics human conversation. When a user inputs a message, the system analyses the context and generates a response that is relevant to the conversation. The use of neural networks and deep learning allows GPT Chat to continuously improve its language generation capabilities, making it more accurate and natural-sounding over time.

However, there are some limitations to the use of neural networks and deep learning in GPT Chat. One of the biggest challenges is the requirement for large amounts of data to train the algorithms effectively. This can be a challenge for smaller businesses or organisations with limited resources. Additionally, the algorithms used in neural networks and deep learning can be complex and difficult to understand, which may require specialised technical expertise to implement and maintain.

Despite these limitations, the use of neural networks and deep learning in GPT Chat has revolutionised the field of natural language processing and opened up new possibilities for businesses looking to improve their customer experience. As these technologies continue to evolve, we can expect to see even more sophisticated language generation capabilities from GPT Chat and other AI-powered chatbot systems.

9

Natural Language Processing

Natural Language Processing (NLP) is an important part of GPT Chat's artificial intelligence technology. It is the field of computer science that focuses on the interaction between human language and computers. NLP enables computers to understand, interpret, and generate human language, which is a critical capability for chatbots like GPT Chat.

NLP involves many different techniques and algorithms, including machine learning and deep learning, to analyse and understand the meaning of language. One of the key challenges of NLP is the complexity of human language, which includes nuances, idioms, and colloquialisms that can be difficult for computers to interpret accurately. However, the development of advanced NLP algorithms has made it possible for machines to understand and generate human-like language with increasing accuracy.

In the context of GPT Chat, NLP is used to interpret the meaning of user input and generate responses that are relevant to the conversation. The system analyses the context of the conversation and uses NLP techniques to identify the most appropriate response based on the user's input. This allows GPT Chat to generate human-like responses that are tailored to the specific needs and interests of the user.

One of the major advantages of NLP in GPT Chat is that it allows for a more natural and seamless conversation between the user and the chatbot. This can lead to increased customer satisfaction and loyalty, as well as improved efficiency for businesses that use chatbots for customer service and support.

However, there are also limitations to the use of NLP in GPT Chat. One challenge is the need for large amounts of data to train the algorithms effectively. This can be particularly challenging for smaller businesses or organisations with limited resources. Additionally, the accuracy of NLP algorithms can be affected by changes in language usage and cultural context, which can require ongoing updates and maintenance to keep the system up-to-date.

Despite these limitations, the use of NLP in GPT Chat has transformed the field of chatbot technology and opened up new possibilities for businesses looking to improve their customer experience. As NLP algorithms continue to improve and evolve, we can expect to see even more advanced and sophisticated chatbot systems in the future.

DATA COLLECTION and training are critical components of GPT Chat's artificial intelligence technology. In order to generate accurate and relevant responses, the system needs to be trained on large amounts of data that reflect real-world conversation patterns and language usage.

The data collection process involves gathering a large corpus of text data that represents the language and conversation patterns of interest. This can include sources such as social media posts, customer support transcripts, and online reviews. The data must be carefully curated and pre-processed to ensure that it is relevant and suitable for training the GPT Chat model.

Once the data has been collected and pre-processed, the training process can begin. This involves using advanced machine learning algorithms to analyse the data and identify patterns and relationships that can be used to generate responses. The training process can take a significant amount of time and computing power, particularly for larger datasets.

One of the key advantages of GPT Chat's training process is that it uses a form of unsupervised learning known as transformer-based language modelling. This approach allows the system to learn patterns and relationships in the data without the need for explicit instructions or supervision.

However, there are also challenges associated with the data collection and training process. One major challenge is the need for large amounts of high-quality data to train the system effectively. This can be particularly challenging for businesses or organisations with limited resources or access to relevant data.

Additionally, the accuracy of the system can be affected by biases in the data, such as language or cultural biases that may be reflected in the training data. It is important to carefully curate and evaluate the data to ensure that it is representative and suitable for the GPT Chat system.

Despite these challenges, the data collection and training process is a critical component of GPT Chat's technology. By carefully curating and analysing large amounts of data, the system can generate accurate and relevant responses that can improve the customer experience and support the needs of businesses and organisations.

10

Gpt 2

GPT-2 is designed to appear as a language generator that can seamlessly blend in with human writing. When given a prompt or starting sentence, the model generates a continuation of the sentence based on its training data. The generated text can range from a few words to multiple paragraphs, depending on the length of the prompt and the complexity of the language.

One of the most impressive aspects of GPT-2's text generation capabilities is its ability to mimic different writing styles and genres. For example, it can generate news articles, scientific reports, and even fiction stories. The model accomplishes this by analyzing the patterns and structures of different types of text data and using them to inform its own language generation.

GPT-2 also uses a technique called unsupervised learning, which means that it does not require explicit instructions or labeling of its training data. Instead, it learns to recognize patterns and relationships in the data on its own, allowing it to adapt to different types of language and writing styles.

Despite its impressive capabilities, GPT-2 is not perfect and still has its limitations. One of the main challenges is ensuring that the generated text is relevant and accurate. The model may sometimes produce nonsensical or inappropriate responses to prompts, especially when the prompt is highly abstract or lacks context.

Furthermore, GPT-2's language generation capabilities require massive amounts of computing power and storage. This makes it inaccessible to most individuals and small businesses without significant financial resources.

Despite these limitations, GPT-2 represents a significant advancement in the field of natural language processing and machine learning. Its ability to generate highly convincing and coherent text has the potential to transform various industries, from content creation to customer service, and beyond.

11

GPT-3

GPT-3 has been dubbed as one of the most advanced and powerful language models ever created. Its incredible natural language generation capabilities have caught the attention of many professionals in various industries, including business, healthcare, education, and entertainment.

One of the most significant differences between GPT-2 and GPT-3 is the amount of data used to train the models. While GPT-2 was trained on a relatively small dataset of 40GB, GPT-3 was trained on an enormous dataset of over 45 terabytes of text, making it one of the largest language models ever created. This massive amount of data allows GPT-3 to generate text that is more contextually relevant and accurate.

GPT-3 is also designed to perform a variety of language-related tasks with little or no additional training. It can perform tasks such as language translation, summarization, and question-answering with impressive accuracy. This is made possible by GPT-3's zero-shot and few-shot learning capabilities, which enable it to learn new tasks without requiring extensive training data.

Moreover, GPT-3 is known for its versatility in handling a wide range of writing styles and genres. It can generate text in different styles, such as formal or casual, and mimic the writing of different authors. It can also generate a range of text types, including news articles, poetry, and even computer code.

Despite its impressive capabilities, GPT-3 still has some limitations. One significant limitation is its tendency to generate biased or inappropriate text, reflecting the biases or inaccuracies in the dataset used to train the model. Additionally, GPT-3 has yet to fully understand the underlying meaning of text, which can lead to confusing or nonsensical outputs.

GPT-3 is undoubtedly a significant milestone in the field of natural language processing and deep learning. Its impressive capabilities have opened up new possibilities for various industries, and many businesses are already exploring ways to integrate GPT-3 into their operations. As technology continues to evolve, it will be exciting to see how GPT-3 can be further developed and applied to real-world problems.

12

GPT-4

GPT-4 is the much-anticipated successor to the widely acclaimed GPT-3 language model. While details about its release and specifications are still scarce, there is already a significant buzz surrounding this upcoming language model.

One of the most significant differences between GPT-4 and its predecessors is the expected increase in the number of parameters used in the model. GPT-3 has 175 billion parameters, making it the largest language model to date. However, GPT-4 is expected to surpass this number significantly, potentially reaching up to a trillion parameters. This increase in parameters will allow for even more powerful and precise natural language generation capabilities.

Another notable feature of GPT-4 is the possibility of incorporating multimodal inputs, such as images or videos, to generate more contextually relevant text. This integration of multiple modes of input can enable the model to generate more accurate and nuanced responses, making it even more versatile and capable than its predecessors.

GPT-4 is also expected to further advance the current state-of-the-art in natural language processing and deep learning by improving upon the limitations of previous models. For example, it may address some of the issues with bias and inconsistency in generated text and improve its understanding of the underlying meaning of text.

However, it is important to note that GPT-4 is not without its potential limitations and challenges. The sheer size of the model can make it computationally expensive and require significant amounts of resources to train and run. Additionally, the integration of multimodal inputs can pose new challenges in data collection and training, potentially requiring even larger datasets.

Despite these challenges, the development of GPT-4 is eagerly anticipated, and its potential impact on the field of natural language processing is expected to be significant. As technology continues to evolve, it is exciting to speculate on the possibilities of what GPT-4 can achieve and the new applications it can enable in various industries.

GPT-4 IS significant for several reasons. Firstly, its potential to have up to a trillion parameters would make it the largest language model in existence, surpassing the current largest model, GPT-3, by a significant margin. This increase in size will enable GPT-4 to generate more accurate and contextually relevant text, making it an even more powerful tool for natural language processing and text generation.

Secondly, the integration of multimodal inputs into the model can significantly expand its capabilities. By incorporating different modes of input such as images, videos, or audio, GPT-4 can generate more nuanced and precise responses, making it a more versatile language model.

Furthermore, GPT-4's development is significant because it is expected to address some of the issues and limitations of previous models. For example, GPT-3 has been criticized for generating biased or inconsistent text, which can have serious implications in certain applications. GPT-4 may be able to mitigate these issues and improve the overall quality and accuracy of the generated text.

Lastly, the development of GPT-4 is significant because it represents the continued advancement of natural language processing and deep learning. As these technologies continue to evolve and improve, they have the potential to revolutionize various industries and applications, from chatbots and virtual assistants to content creation and translation.

13

Why gpt 4 is better than gpt 3?

GPT-4: The Next Generation of AI Text Generation

As the field of natural language processing continues to advance, the latest breakthrough is the development of GPT-4, the fourth iteration of OpenAI's Generative Pre-trained Transformer model. GPT-4 is expected to be a significant improvement over its predecessor, GPT-3, and will have a number of new features and capabilities.

GPT-4 is expected to have a significantly larger number of parameters than GPT-3, which means it will require more computational power to run. However, with advancements in computing technology, GPT-4 will be able to handle more complex tasks and generate more accurate responses.

One of the most significant improvements of GPT-4 is its multilingual capabilities. While GPT-3 can generate text in multiple languages, it is not truly multilingual. GPT-4 is expected to have true multilingual capabilities, allowing it to generate high-quality text in multiple languages simultaneously.

Another key feature of GPT-4 is its improved understanding of context. GPT-4 is expected to have a better understanding of context and the ability to generate more coherent and natural-sounding responses. This is due to the improved training data and the incorporation of more advanced machine learning techniques.

GPT-4 is expected to have a larger and more sophisticated memory system, allowing it to retain more information and make more informed decisions. This could lead to improved natural language processing and better text generation.

GPT-4 is expected to be better integrated with other AI systems, such as computer vision and speech recognition. This could lead to new applications and use cases, such as generating captions for images and videos.

Overall, GPT-4 represents a significant step forward in the field of natural language processing and AI text generation. Its improved computational power, true multilingual capabilities, enhanced understanding of context, better memory, and improved integration with other AI systems make it an exciting development for businesses and individuals looking to leverage AI technology for their text generation needs.

14

Business case use of Gpt Chat

The use of artificial intelligence (AI) in business has increased significantly over the years. One of the most popular applications of AI in the realm of customer service is chatbots. These chatbots provide quick and efficient responses to customer inquiries, but they have limitations when it comes to understanding and responding to complex language and providing personalised responses. This is where GPT (Generative Pre-trained Transformer) chat comes in.

GPT chat is a type of AI language model that uses deep learning algorithms to generate human-like text based on the context provided. With its advanced natural language processing capabilities, GPT chat can understand and respond to complex language, making it ideal for use in customer service and other business applications.

In this article, we will explore the business case for using GPT chat, including its benefits, potential use cases, and implementation considerations.

GPT chat provides several benefits to businesses. Some of the key benefits include:

1. Improved Customer Satisfaction

GPT chat can provide personalised, human-like responses to

customer inquiries, leading to a more positive customer experience. By understanding the context of the customer's inquiry, GPT chat can provide accurate and relevant responses, which can help build trust and confidence with the customer.

1. Increased Efficiency

GPT chat can handle multiple customer inquiries simultaneously, reducing the workload on human customer service representatives and speeding up response times. This can help businesses provide quick and efficient support to customers, which can improve customer satisfaction.

1. Cost Savings

By automating certain customer service tasks, businesses can reduce the need for human customer service representatives, resulting in cost savings. GPT chat can handle common customer inquiries, which can free up human representatives to handle more complex inquiries.

1. Data Insights

GPT chat can collect data on customer inquiries and responses, providing valuable insights into customer needs and preferences. This data can be used to improve products and services, as well as to tailor marketing and sales efforts to better meet customer needs.

Use Cases for GPT Chat

GPT chat can be used in a variety of business contexts. Some potential use cases include:

1. Customer Service

GPT chat can handle customer inquiries and provide support for common issues, such as order tracking, product information, and technical troubleshooting. GPT chat can also be used to provide support outside of regular business hours, which can improve customer satisfaction and reduce response times.

1. Sales and Marketing

GPT chat can engage with potential customers, provide product recommendations, and even process sales transactions. This can help businesses reach new customers and increase sales while providing personalised support to customers.

1. HR and Recruiting

GPT chat can assist with onboarding new employees, answer common HR-related questions, and even conduct initial job interviews. This can help businesses streamline their HR processes and reduce the workload on human HR representatives.

1. Financial Services

GPT chat can provide financial advice, answer questions about account balances, and even help customers with financial planning. This can help financial services companies provide personalised support to customers while reducing the workload on human representatives.

Implementation Considerations

When implementing GPT chat in a business context, there are several considerations to keep in mind. These include:

1. Integration

GPT chat will need to be integrated with existing business systems, such as CRM and ticketing systems, to ensure a seamless customer experience. Integration can also help businesses collect data on customer inquiries and responses, which can be used to improve products and services.

1. Training

GPT chat will need to be trained on business-specific language and customer inquiries to provide accurate and relevant responses. This training can be done using historical data or by providing feedback to the GPT chat system as it interacts with customers.

1. Data Privacy and Security

GPT chat will need to comply with data privacy and security regulations, such as GDPR and CCPA, to ensure customer data is protected. Businesses will need to implement appropriate security measures to protect the GPT chat system from cyber threats and data breaches.

1. Maintenance and Updates

GPT CHAT WILL REQUIRE ongoing maintenance and updates to ensure it continues to provide accurate and relevant responses. Businesses will need to have a plan in place for monitoring and maintaining the GPT chat system, including updating it with new language models and responding to feedback from customers.

GPT CHAT PROVIDES several benefits to businesses, including improved customer satisfaction, increased efficiency, cost savings, and data insights. It can be used in a variety of business contexts, including customer service, sales and marketing, HR and recruiting, and financial services. When implementing GPT chat, businesses should consider integration, training, data privacy and security, and ongoing maintenance and updates. With careful planning and implementation, GPT chat can be a powerful tool for businesses looking to improve their customer service and operational efficiency.

EXAMPLE:

ALICE HAD BEEN RUNNING her online store for several years now, and she was proud of the high-quality products and services she provided to her customers. However, she knew that her customer service could be improved, especially during peak sales periods when customer inquiries and support requests increased.

Alice had heard about GPT chat and how it could be used to provide efficient and accurate customer service. Intrigued, she began researching the technology and exploring how it could be integrated into her business.

After defining her use case and goals, Alice chose a GPT chat provider that met her business needs and was easy to integrate with her existing systems. She worked with her development team to ensure a seamless integration that would provide a smooth customer experience.

The next step was to train the GPT chat on business-specific language and customer inquiries. Alice provided historical data and feedback to the GPT chat system, ensuring it was able to accurately and efficiently respond to customer inquiries.

Data privacy and security were also a priority for Alice, and she worked with her team to implement appropriate security measures to protect the GPT chat system from cyber threats and data breaches. Alice knew that her customers' data was critical to the success of her business, and she wanted to ensure it was protected at all times.

Alice also monitored and maintained the GPT chat system, continually refining the training data and updating the system with new language models. As a result, her customers enjoyed a faster, more efficient support experience, and Alice was able to reduce the workload on her human customer service representatives.

Alice's implementation of GPT chat for customer service proved to be a powerful tool for improving her customer service and operational efficiency. By taking the time to carefully plan and implement the technology, Alice was able to provide her customers with a better experience and increase the overall success of her online store.

As businesses continue to seek ways to improve their customer service and operational efficiency, GPT chat is emerging as a valuable tool. By defining use cases and goals, choosing the right GPT chat provider, integrating the system with existing business systems, training the GPT chat on business-specific language and inquiries, implementing data privacy and security measures, and monitoring and maintaining the system, businesses can harness the power of

GPT chat to improve their customer service and increase their bottom line.

ANOTHER EXAMPLE ABOUT FREELANCER:

AS A FREELANCE WRITER, John had a steady flow of clients, but he struggled to keep up with the demands of managing multiple projects and deadlines simultaneously. He often found himself spending more time communicating with clients and managing revisions than actually writing.

One day, John came across the concept of using GPT chat to automate some of his client communication tasks. Intrigued, he began researching the technology and exploring how it could be integrated into his freelance writing business.

After defining his use case and goals, John chose a GPT chat provider that met his business needs and was easy to integrate with his existing systems. He worked with his development team to ensure a seamless integration that would provide a smooth experience for his clients.

The next step was to train the GPT chat on business-specific language and inquiries. John provided historical data and feedback to the GPT chat system, ensuring it was able to accurately and efficiently respond to client inquiries about project status, revisions, and other common topics.

John also integrated the GPT chat system with his project management software, allowing the system to automatically send notifications to clients when a milestone had been completed or a new revision was available.

Data privacy and security were also a priority for John, and he worked with his team to implement appropriate security measures to protect the GPT chat system from cyber threats and data breaches. John knew that his clients' data was critical to the success of his business, and he wanted to ensure it was protected at all times.

Finally, John monitored and maintained the GPT chat system, continually refining the training data and updating the system with new language models. As a result, he was able to spend more time writing and less time managing client communication, leading to increased productivity and profitability.

In conclusion, John's implementation of GPT chat for client communication proved to be a valuable tool for improving his productivity and overall success as a freelance writer. By defining use cases and goals, choosing the right GPT chat provider, integrating the system with existing business systems, training the GPT chat on business-specific language and inquiries, implementing data privacy and security measures, and monitoring and maintaining the system, freelancers can harness the power of GPT chat to automate routine communication tasks and focus on delivering high-quality work to their clients.

15

20 Best Cases to Use Gpt Chat

1. Create great content in seconds. It have never been so easy!

CREATING great content using GPT Chat involves the following steps:

1. Define your topic and target audience: Knowing your audience and topic will help you generate content that resonates with your readers.
2. Use a reliable GPT Chat platform: Choose a GPT Chat platform with a high level of accuracy and performance.
3. Provide clear and concise prompts: Give specific prompts that will guide the AI to generate the right content.
4. Edit and refine the generated content: Review the content generated by GPT Chat, and make necessary edits to ensure it meets your standards.
5. Add your personal touch: Inject your personality and style into the content to make it unique and engaging.

BY FOLLOWING THESE STEPS, you can use GPT Chat to create high-quality content that resonates with your target audience.

HERE ARE 10 best prompts for content creation:

SURE, here are 10 best prompts to use when creating content using GPT Chat:

1. "Write a blog post about the benefits of using [product/service]."
2. "Create a social media post highlighting the features of our latest [product/service]."
3. "Craft a persuasive email promoting our [product/service] to potential customers."
4. "Write an informative article on the impact of [current event/topic] on [industry/field]."
5. "Create a product description that effectively communicates the value of our [product/service]."
6. "Write a how-to guide on [task/process] that's easy to follow and understand."
7. "Create a landing page that highlights the key benefits of our [product/service]."
8. "Write an engaging script for a promotional video showcasing our [product/service]."
9. "Craft a press release announcing our latest partnership/acquisition/product launch."
10. "Write a case study that demonstrates the positive results achieved by our [product/service] for a specific client/customer."

2. **Mental health support: Use GPT chat to receive personalised mental health support and guidance.**

. . .

CHAT GPT FOR BEGINNERS

IN TIMES OF NEED, GPT chat can be a reliable and accessible source of guidance and support for your mental health. To make the most of this resource, it's important to follow a few steps:

Firstly, look for a reputable platform that specialises in mental health support and utilises GPT technology. Once you've registered or signed up, share some basic information about yourself and your mental health history.

Then, start a conversation with the chatbot and describe your concerns or issues in an honest and open manner. The GPT chatbot will ask questions to better understand your situation and provide personalised guidance and support, which may include coping strategies or self-care practices.

It's important to engage with the chatbot regularly, track your progress, and communicate any changes or concerns you may have. However, it's also important to recognise that GPT chat is not a substitute for professional mental health care. In cases of severe or persistent mental health issues, it's crucial to seek help from a licensed professional, and GPT chat can serve as a helpful supplement to traditional mental health care.

10 BEST PROMPTS to use for your mental health :

1. Can you recommend some techniques to manage stress and anxiety?
2. How can I better cope with depression?
3. What are some ways to practice self-care for better mental health?
4. Can you suggest some online resources or support groups for mental health?
5. How can I improve my sleep quality to support my mental well-being?
6. Can you provide some mindfulness exercises to help with relaxation?
7. What are some ways to reduce negative thinking patterns?
8. How can I overcome social anxiety in social situations?

9. Can you recommend some strategies to boost self-esteem and confidence?
10. What are some healthy habits or lifestyle changes that can support mental health?

3. Virtual personal shopping assistant: Use GPT chat to receive personalized product recommendations and assistance with online shopping.

As a customer, GPT chat can help you with virtual personal shopping assistance by providing the following benefits:

1. Personalised product recommendations: GPT chat can understand your preferences and shopping behaviour, and provide personalised product recommendations that fit your needs and tastes.

1. Quick and convenient assistance: With GPT chat, you can get quick and convenient assistance with your online shopping needs without having to wait on hold or navigate a complicated customer service system.

1. Answering product questions: GPT chat can help answer any questions you may have about a product or service, such as its features, benefits, or pricing, helping you make informed decisions about your purchase.
2. Post-purchase assistance: In case of any issues or concerns, GPT chat can provide you with personalised support for returns, exchanges, or any other post-purchase assistance.

HERE ARE prompts for this case:

1. What are you looking to buy today? Let me help you find the perfect product based on your preferences and needs.
2. Do you have a specific brand in mind? I can provide recommendations on similar products and alternatives that may better suit your preferences.
3. Are you shopping for a specific occasion or event? Let me suggest some products that will help you stand out and make a great impression.
4. Are you on a tight budget? I can recommend affordable products that still meet your preferences and needs.
5. Do you need help finding the right size or fit? Let me assist you in finding products that match your measurements and style.
6. Have you considered any accessories or complementary products? Let me suggest some products that will complete your look and enhance your experience.
7. Would you like to see some products that are currently trending? Let me show you some of the latest and most popular items in your preferred category.
8. Do you have any ethical or environmental concerns? Let me suggest some products that align with your values and beliefs.
9. Have you shopped with us before? Let me show you some products that you may have missed since your last visit.
10. Would you like me to create a personalised shopping list for you? Let me suggest products based on your preferences and needs, and save them for future reference.

4. Writing letters to customers

Writing letters to customers is an essential aspect of customer service. It's an opportunity to build a relationship with your customers, communicate important information, and address their concerns. Whether it's a thank you letter, an apology letter, or a letter providing an update on a product or service, it's essential to ensure that the letter is clear, concise, and professional.

When writing a letter to a customer, it's important to consider the tone, language, and content. The tone should be friendly, polite, and professional. Use language that is easy to understand, and avoid using technical jargon. The content of the letter should be specific and relevant to the customer's needs.

Before writing the letter, it's important to gather all the necessary information, such as the customer's name, address, and order number. This information helps to personalise the letter and make the customer feel valued. It's also important to proofread the letter to ensure that there are no grammatical errors or typos.

By taking the time to write a well-crafted letter, you can show your customers that you value their business and are committed to providing excellent customer service. With the help of GPT Chat, you can streamline the process of writing letters and save time while still providing personalised and professional communication to your customers.

USING GPT Chat for customer letters involves the following steps:

1. Define the purpose and tone of the letter: Determine the type of letter you want to send and the tone you want to use. For instance, if you want to send a complaint letter, the tone will be different from a thank you letter.
2. Use a reliable GPT Chat platform: Choose a GPT Chat platform with a high level of accuracy and performance to generate the letter.
3. Provide clear and concise prompts: Give specific prompts that will guide the AI to generate the right content. For example, you can provide the customer's name, the order number, and other relevant details.
4. Review and edit the generated letter: Review the letter generated by GPT Chat, and make necessary edits to ensure it meets your standards. Ensure that the tone is appropriate for the purpose of the letter.

5. Add your personal touch: Inject your personality and style into the letter to make it feel more personalised and genuine.
6. Send the letter: Once you are satisfied with the letter, you can send it to the customer.

By following these steps, you can use GPT Chat to generate customer letters that are personalised, informative, and engaging.

5. Personalized nutrition and meal planning: Use GPT chat to receive personalized nutrition and meal planning advice.

GPT chat can be an excellent tool for receiving personalised nutrition and meal planning advice. By using natural language processing, GPT chat can understand your dietary preferences, restrictions, and health goals. Based on this information, GPT chat can provide personalised nutrition and meal planning advice, including meal ideas, recipes, and ingredient substitutions. GPT chat can also suggest ways to optimise your diet for specific health conditions, such as diabetes or high blood pressure. Additionally, GPT chat can answer any questions you may have about nutrition, such as how to incorporate more plant-based foods into your diet or how to ensure you are getting enough protein. With the help of GPT chat, you can create a personalised nutrition plan that fits your dietary needs and lifestyle.

SOME POTENTIAL GPT chat prompts related to personalised nutrition and meal planning:

- What are some healthy meal options for someone who is trying to lose weight?
- Can you suggest some vegetarian sources of protein for someone who is looking to build muscle?
- What are some easy and healthy snacks I can bring to work?
- Can you recommend some low-carb meal options for someone with diabetes?
- What should I eat before and after a workout?

- I have food allergies/sensitivities - can you suggest some meal options that would work for me?
- Can you provide a personalised meal plan based on my dietary restrictions and fitness goals?
- What are some healthy meal prep ideas for someone with a busy schedule?
- Can you suggest some healthy dessert options that won't ruin my diet?
- I'm trying to eat more plant-based - can you suggest some meal options that are both healthy and flavourful?

6. Virtual personal stylist: Use GPT chat to receive personalized fashion advice and recommendations.

Incorporating GPT chat into your fashion routine can provide you with a virtual personal stylist. Here are several ways GPT chat can offer personalised fashion advice and recommendations:

Understanding your fashion preferences: By utilising natural language processing, GPT chat can understand your fashion preferences, such as your favourite colours, patterns, and clothing styles. Based on your preferences, GPT chat can provide tailored fashion advice and recommendations.

Providing fashion recommendations: GPT chat can provide recommendations for clothing items, accessories, and outfits based on your style preferences, body type, and occasion. Additionally, GPT chat can suggest where to shop for specific items.

Assisting with outfit selection: GPT chat can help you choose outfits for various occasions, including job interviews or nights out. GPT chat can also give advice on how to mix and match clothing items to create unique outfits.

Answering fashion-related questions: GPT chat can answer any questions you may have about fashion, such as how to dress for a specific body type, how to incorporate new trends into your wardrobe, or how to accessorise an outfit.

Providing personalised style tips: GPT chat can give personalised style advice based on your preferences and body type. Furthermore,

CHAT GPT FOR BEGINNERS

GPT chat can advise on dressing for different seasons, climates, and events.

PROMPTS to start using GPT Chat as you personal stylist :

1. "Hi there! What are you looking for today? Let me help you find the perfect outfit based on your personal style."
2. "What's the occasion? Let's find you an outfit that suits the event and makes you feel confident."
3. "Do you have a specific item in mind that you want to build an outfit around? I can suggest some pieces that will complement it perfectly."
4. "Let's talk about your body type and how to highlight your best features. I can suggest clothing styles that will flatter your figure."
5. "What colours do you like to wear? I can suggest items that will match your preferences and skin tone."
6. "Are you looking for something specific, like sustainable or ethical fashion? I can suggest brands and items that fit your values."
7. "Do you need help accessorising your outfit? Let me suggest some jewellery, bags, or shoes that will complete your look."
8. "Let's create a virtual wardrobe for you. I can suggest staple pieces and versatile items that you can mix and match for different outfits."
9. "Are you unsure how to style a particular piece of clothing? Let me suggest some outfit ideas that will inspire you."
10. "What's your budget for this shopping trip? I can suggest items that fit within your price range and offer the best value for your money."

7. Personalized interior design advice: Use GPT chat to receive personalized interior design advice and recommendations.

Looking for personalised interior design advice and recommendations? Look no further than GPT chat! Here are just a few ways this innovative tool can help transform your space:

- Understanding your design preferences: With its powerful natural language processing, GPT chat can quickly and easily understand your design preferences, from colour schemes and furniture styles to decor elements and more. Armed with this knowledge, GPT chat can provide tailored advice and recommendations that perfectly match your unique tastes.
- Providing design recommendations: From furniture pieces and decor elements to colour schemes and more, GPT chat can suggest a wide range of design recommendations based on your preferences, budget, and room layout. Whether you're looking for a classic look or a modern twist, GPT chat can help you achieve the perfect design style for your space.
- Helping with room layout: Struggling to make the most of your available space? GPT chat can help! By providing expert advice on room layout, furniture arrangement, and more, GPT chat can help you maximise both the functionality and aesthetic appeal of your room.
- Answering design-related questions: Have a specific design question or concern? GPT chat has you covered! Whether you're wondering how to incorporate a specific colour into your design scheme or how to create a focal point in a room, GPT chat can provide the answers you need.
- Providing personalised design tips: Looking for even more personalised design advice? GPT chat can offer tips and suggestions that are tailored to your unique preferences and room layout. With its expert guidance, you can create a space that perfectly reflects your individual style and personality.

CHAT GPT FOR BEGINNERS

PROMPTS FOR THIS CHAPTER:

1. Start by describing your design preferences to the GPT chatbot, such as your preferred colour schemes, furniture styles, and decor elements.
2. Ask the chatbot for recommendations on furniture pieces, decor elements, and colour schemes based on your design preferences, room layout, and budget.
3. Seek advice from the chatbot on how to create a cohesive and visually appealing design by arranging furniture and decor elements in a specific way.
4. Ask the chatbot for suggestions on how to maximise space and functionality in a room, and how to create a specific mood or atmosphere.
5. Provide the chatbot with pictures or measurements of your space, and ask for design tips that are tailored to your specific room layout.
6. Seek inspiration and ideas from the chatbot on different design styles and themes that may suit your preferences.
7. Ask the chatbot for advice on incorporating a specific colour into your design scheme or mixing and matching different design styles.
8. Seek guidance from the chatbot on how to create a focal point in a room, such as through artwork or lighting.
9. Get recommendations from the chatbot on where to shop for specific furniture or decor items that fit within your design preferences and budget.
10. Follow up with the chatbot regularly and communicate any changes or concerns, and keep track of your progress as you implement its personalised design advice.

8. Making money using ChatGPT

Are you looking for ways to make some extra cash without investing too much time and effort? Look no further, because with the help of online resources like ChatGPT, you can discover side hustles and gigs that fit your skills and interests. This guide will provide you with some simple steps to help you find out how to make money easily using ChatGPT and other resources.

First, conduct online research by using search engines to look for articles, blogs, and forums that discuss ways to make money easily. You can search for keywords like "easy ways to make money," "side hustles," or "online jobs." Then, leverage ChatGPT to get information and ideas on how to make money easily. Ask questions like "What are some easy ways to make money online?" or "What are some side hustles that require minimal effort?"

Next, evaluate your skills and interests to identify opportunities that align with them. For example, if you enjoy writing, look for freelance writing opportunities. Additionally, check your local classified ads, bulletin boards, and community websites for job openings, gigs, or other opportunities to make money.

Finally, consider using online platforms like online marketplaces, survey sites, and paid content creation sites. Remember that while there are many opportunities to make money easily, many require effort and dedication. Therefore, it's essential to do your research, evaluate your options, and choose the best ones that align with your skills, interests, and goals.

HERE ARE some prompts that might help you :

1. What are some easy ways to make money online?
2. How can I earn extra income without investing too much time or effort?
3. What are some side hustles that require minimal effort?
4. How can I use ChatGPT to find opportunities to make money?
5. What are some platforms that allow me to make money easily?
6. How can I monetise my skills and interests to earn extra income?

7. Are there any legitimate work-from-home opportunities that I can explore?
8. How can I identify and avoid scams when looking for ways to make money easily?
9. What are some tips for managing my finances and saving money while earning extra income?
10. How can I balance my full-time job and my side hustle to ensure that I am productive and efficient?

9. Planning a trip

Embarking on a trip can be a thrilling adventure, but it can also be an overwhelming task. From deciding on the best itinerary to finding the best deals on flights and accommodations, there's a lot to consider. Fortunately, GPT Chat can be your ultimate travel buddy, making the planning process easier and more efficient.

Here are some ways GPT Chat can assist you with planning your trip:

- It can help you brainstorm ideas for your trip. With GPT Chat, you can get recommendations on the best places to visit, things to do, and restaurants to try. Simply tell GPT Chat about your preferences and interests, and it can generate a list of suggestions tailored to your needs.
- It can help you find the best deals on flights and accommodations. GPT Chat can search through various travel websites to find the best deals on flights and accommodations that match your specific requirements and preferences.
- It can help you create a personalised itinerary. With GPT Chat, you can create a custom itinerary based on your preferences and interests. Just provide some information about your trip, such as your destination, travel dates, and interests, and GPT Chat can generate a personalised itinerary that includes the best places to visit, things to do, and restaurants to try.
- It can help you navigate your destination. Once you arrive

at your destination, GPT Chat can provide recommendations for nearby attractions, restaurants, and activities. Additionally, it can assist you in navigating the area by providing directions, transportation options, and other helpful information.

Overall, GPT Chat can be a valuable travel companion, offering assistance and support throughout the planning and execution of your trip. Whether you're a seasoned traveler or a novice explorer, GPT Chat can help make your journey smoother and more enjoyable.

HERE ARE some prompts for travel planning:

1. How can GPT Chat help me find the best deals on flights and accommodations for my trip?
2. Can GPT Chat help me create a customised itinerary for my trip based on my interests and preferences?
3. What kind of information should I provide to GPT Chat to help it generate the best recommendations for my trip?
4. Can GPT Chat provide me with directions and other useful information for navigating my destination?
5. How can I ensure that the recommendations provided by GPT Chat are accurate and reliable?
6. Are there any potential limitations or biases with using GPT Chat for trip planning?
7. Can GPT Chat recommend off-the-beaten-path destinations or activities that I may not have considered on my own?
8. How can I incorporate GPT Chat into my existing trip planning process?
9. What are some examples of successful trip planning using GPT Chat?
10. Can GPT Chat assist me with making reservations and bookings for my trip?

10. Creating applications

GPT Chat is a versatile tool that can help developers in various ways while creating applications. It can generate ideas for new applications based on user input, design user interfaces that are user-friendly and visually appealing, generate high-quality content tailored to the specific needs of the application, identify bugs and suggest improvements to enhance the overall performance and reliability of the application, and provide customer support by understanding user queries and providing helpful responses. By leveraging machine learning algorithms and natural language processing, GPT Chat can streamline the development process and improve the overall user experience of the application.

SOME PROMPTS you might be interested in:

1. How can GPT Chat help in developing user personas for my application?
2. Can GPT Chat assist in creating wireframes and prototypes for my application?
3. How can GPT Chat help in identifying potential features and functionality that users may want in my application?
4. Can GPT Chat suggest ways to optimise the user interface and improve overall user experience in my application?
5. How can GPT Chat assist in creating documentation for my application, such as user manuals and help files?
6. Can GPT Chat suggest ways to improve the performance and scalability of my application?
7. How can GPT Chat assist in conducting user testing and gathering feedback for my application?
8. Can GPT Chat help in creating marketing materials and promotional content for my application?
9. How can GPT Chat assist in identifying potential security vulnerabilities in my application?
10. Can GPT Chat suggest ways to integrate artificial

intelligence and machine learning into my application to enhance functionality and performance?

11. Virtual study buddy: Use GPT chat to connect with other students and receive study tips and guidance.

In today's technology-driven world, students have a new study buddy: GPT Chat. This powerful tool provides assistance and support in a variety of ways, helping students to excel in their academic pursuits. Whether it's homework help, study sessions, note-taking, research assistance, writing assistance, time management, or motivation, GPT Chat is there to lend a helping hand.

With GPT Chat, students can get instant feedback and guidance on difficult homework assignments, improving their comprehension and retention of the material. Additionally, GPT Chat can serve as a study partner, quizzing students on topics and testing their knowledge, further enhancing their understanding and retention of the material.

GPT Chat can also help students take better notes, providing summaries and key takeaways from lectures and readings to help them stay organised and retain important information. Furthermore, when it comes to research, GPT Chat can save students time by providing relevant articles and resources on specific topics, helping them find credible sources for their assignments.

In addition, GPT Chat can help students improve their writing skills by providing suggestions and feedback on their essays and papers, improving their grammar, syntax, and overall writing style. GPT Chat can also assist students in managing their time effectively by providing reminders and setting schedules for study sessions and assignments.

Finally, GPT Chat can serve as a source of motivation and encouragement for students, helping them stay focused and on track with their studies. In summary, GPT Chat is an invaluable virtual study buddy, providing support and assistance to students in various aspects of their academic journey.

HERE ARE some prompts that might be helpful for this case:

1. How can GPT Chat help me study more effectively and efficiently?
2. Can GPT Chat assist me in organising my study schedule and setting goals?
3. How can GPT Chat help me improve my note-taking skills and retain important information?
4. Can GPT Chat suggest resources and materials to help me better understand difficult concepts?
5. How can GPT Chat assist me in writing essays and papers for my classes?
6. Can GPT Chat help me prepare for exams and quizzes by quizzing me on the material?
7. How can GPT Chat assist me in conducting research for my assignments?
8. Can GPT Chat provide me with study tips and strategies for specific subjects?
9. How can GPT Chat help me stay motivated and on track with my studies?
10. Can GPT Chat assist me in collaborating with other students and creating study groups?

12. **Personalized career coaching:** Use GPT chat to receive personalized career coaching and job search advice.

Imagine having a powerful tool at your fingertips that can provide you with personalised career coaching and job search advice. This tool exists in the form of GPT chat, and here's how you can use it to your advantage:

First, find a GPT chat platform that offers career coaching and job search advice. Many platforms use GPT technology to offer tailored advice based on your specific needs and preferences.

Next, introduce yourself to the virtual assistant and share your career goals and the type of job you're seeking. The assistant will ask you questions to better understand your skills, experience, and aspirations. Provide honest answers and as much information as possible so that the assistant can provide personalised career advice.

The virtual assistant will provide you with customised career advice based on your skills and career goals, including tips on job search strategies, resume writing, interview preparation, and career development.

If you have any questions about the advice provided, don't hesitate to ask for clarification or additional information. The virtual assistant is there to help you.

Finally, it's up to you to implement the advice provided by the virtual assistant. Use the advice to improve your job search strategies and career development, and increase your chances of finding the right job.

By following these steps, you can take advantage of GPT chat as a powerful tool for personalised career coaching and job search advice. Best of luck on your job search journey!

HERE ARE some GPT chat prompts that can be used for this chapter on using GPT chat as a virtual writing assistant:

1. What are some common writing challenges that you've faced in the past, and how have you overcome them?
2. What are some specific writing projects that you're currently working on, and what kind of assistance do you need to make them more effective?
3. What kind of writing prompts do you find most helpful in sparking your creativity and generating new ideas?
4. How can writing tools like grammar and spell checkers help you improve the quality of your writing, and what strategies can you use to make the most of these tools?
5. In what ways can GPT chat technology be used to provide personalised writing advice and assistance, and how can you make the most of this resource to achieve your writing goals?
6. Have you used GPT chat as a virtual writing assistant before? If so, what was your experience like, and what did you find most helpful about the tool?
7. What kind of feedback do you typically receive on your writing, and how can you use GPT chat to

address areas of improvement and build on your strengths?
8. How can GPT chat help you overcome writer's block and maintain momentum on your writing projects, and what strategies can you use to stay focused and productive?

13. Virtual writing assistant: Use GPT chat to receive writing advice and assistance.

As you embark on your writing journey, a virtual writing assistant using GPT chat can serve as a valuable resource to help you improve your skills and refine your craft. By finding a GPT chat platform and introducing yourself to the virtual assistant, you can receive personalised writing advice and assistance tailored to your specific needs. Sharing writing samples with the assistant allows it to better understand your writing style and provide tailored advice on grammar, punctuation, sentence structure, tone, and style. By taking advantage of the writing tools offered by the platform, such as grammar and spell checkers, writing prompts, and word choice suggestions, you can further enhance your writing skills. With diligent implementation of the advice provided by the virtual assistant, you can achieve you're writing goals and become a more effective and confident writer.

As you embark on your writing journey, a virtual writing assistant using GPT chat can serve as a valuable resource to help you improve your skills and refine your craft. By finding a GPT chat platform and introducing yourself to the virtual assistant, you can receive personalised writing advice and assistance tailored to your specific needs. Sharing writing samples with the assistant allows it to better understand your writing style and provide tailored advice on grammar, punctuation, sentence structure, tone, and style.

With the help of writing prompts, you can also spark your creativity and overcome writer's block. Many GPT chat platforms offer a variety of prompts that can help you generate ideas and inspiration for your writing projects. Whether you're working on a novel, a blog post, or a research paper, the prompts can help you explore new perspectives and approaches to your writing.

By taking advantage of the writing tools offered by the platform, such as grammar and spell checkers, you can also ensure that your writing is error-free and polished. These tools can help you identify and correct common mistakes, improve your writing style, and enhance the overall quality of your work.

With diligent implementation of the advice provided by the virtual assistant, and by using the prompts and writing tools offered by the platform, you can achieve you're writing goals and become a more effective and confident writer. So, don't hesitate to leverage the power of GPT chat as a virtual writing assistant to take your writing skills to the next level!

HERE ARE some GPT chat prompts that can be used for this chapter on using GPT chat as a virtual writing assistant:

1. "Can you provide me with feedback on the grammar and punctuation in this paragraph?"
2. "I'm having trouble with the sentence structure in this section. Can you provide some suggestions?"
3. "I want to make sure my writing has the right tone. Can you help me with that?"
4. "I'm struggling to find the right words to convey my message. Can you assist with vocabulary suggestions?"
5. "I want to make sure my writing style is consistent throughout my document. Can you provide some tips?"
6. "Can you help me rephrase this sentence to make it more concise and clear?"
7. "I'm not sure if this paragraph flows well. Can you provide feedback on the coherence and organization?"
8. "I want to improve my writing skills. Can you provide me with some resources or exercises?"
9. "Can you assist with formatting and layout suggestions for this document?"
10. "I need to write for a specific audience. Can you help me tailor my writing to their preferences and expectations?"

14. Virtual legal advice: Use GPT chat to receive personalized legal advice and guidance.

As an AI language model, GPT chat can provide general information and guidance related to legal matters, but it is important to note that it is not a substitute for licensed legal advice. This chapter will guide you on how to use GPT chat to receive personalised legal advice and guidance.

To begin, type in your legal question or concern with as much detail as possible to receive the most accurate information. GPT chat will generate a response based on your query, and may also ask follow-up questions to better understand your situation. Additionally, GPT chat can provide general information about relevant laws and regulations in your jurisdiction.

It is important to keep in mind that the information provided by GPT chat is for educational and informational purposes only, and should not be interpreted as legal advice. It is always recommended to consult a licensed attorney for personalised legal advice.

If further assistance is required, GPT chat can help you find and connect with licensed attorneys in your area who specialise in the relevant area of law.

In summary, while GPT chat can provide general guidance, it is not a substitute for professional legal advice. This chapter will help you understand how to use GPT chat to receive personalised legal advice and guidance, and provide insight into the limitations of its capabilities.

HERE'S an example conversation that demonstrates how to use GPT chat for personalised legal advice and guidance:

User: Hi, I have a legal question about starting a business in California. Can you help me?

GPT chat: Of course! What specific legal concerns do you have regarding starting a business in California?

User: I'm not sure where to start with the legal paperwork and requirements. What do I need to do to register my business?

GPT chat: To register your business in California, you will need to file the appropriate paperwork with the California Secretary of State's office. This includes filing articles of incorporation or organisation, and obtaining any necessary licenses and permits.

User: That sounds complicated. Can you help me with the paperwork?

GPT chat: While I can provide general information about the paperwork required to register a business in California, I cannot fill out the forms for you or provide personalised legal advice. It's best to consult with a licensed attorney or business formation service to ensure that everything is completed correctly.

User: Okay, thanks for the information. Are there any other legal requirements I need to be aware of?

GPT chat: Yes, there are several other legal requirements you should be aware of when starting a business in California, including tax obligations, employment laws, and zoning regulations. I can provide you with general information on these topics, but it's important to consult a licensed attorney for personalised legal advice.

User: Okay, thanks for your help. How can I find a licensed attorney who specialises in business law in California?

GPT chat: You can search for attorneys on the California State Bar website, or you can use online legal directories such as Avvo or Legal-Zoom to find attorneys in your area who specialise in business law.

HERE ARE some prompts you can use to initiate a conversation with GPT chat for personalised legal advice and guidance:

1. "Hi, I have a legal question about [insert your legal concern]. Can you help me?"
2. "I need help understanding [insert a specific law or regulation]. Can you provide me with some guidance?"
3. "I'm not sure what legal paperwork I need to file for [insert your specific legal matter]. Can you provide me with some information?"
4. "I need to find a licensed attorney who specialises in [insert your specific legal matter]. Can you help me find one?"
5. "I'm facing a legal issue with [insert your specific legal matter]. What should I do next?"

REMEMBER, the more specific and detailed your question or concern is, the more accurate and helpful the information GPT chat can provide. And always keep in mind that GPT chat is not a substitute for professional legal advice, and it's always recommended to consult a licensed attorney for personalised legal advice

15. Virtual financial advice: Use GPT chat to receive personalized financial advice and guidance.

As an AI language model, I can offer guidance and general information on a wide range of financial matters. While I cannot provide personalised financial advice, I can help answer general questions and provide educational resources to help you make informed financial decisions. Here are some common financial issues where GPT chat may be helpful:

1. Debt management: If you are struggling with debt, GPT chat can help you explore options for getting out of debt, such as debt consolidation, debt settlement, or bankruptcy.
2. Budgeting: If you need help creating a budget or managing your expenses, GPT chat can offer guidance on creating a budget that works for your unique financial situation and help you identify areas where you can cut expenses.
3. Retirement planning: If you are planning for retirement, GPT chat can help you understand retirement savings options such as 401(k)s, IRAs, and other investment vehicles.
4. Investing: If you want to learn more about investing, GPT chat can help you understand basic investment concepts such as stocks, bonds, mutual funds, and ETFs.
5. Insurance: If you have questions about insurance, such as whether you need life insurance, auto insurance, or homeowners insurance, GPT chat can help you understand the different types of insurance and how they work.
6. Tax planning: If you need help with tax planning, GPT

chat can help you understand different tax deductions and credits that may be available to you.
7. Financial planning: If you need help developing a comprehensive financial plan, GPT chat can help you understand the steps involved in creating a plan and provide resources to help you get started.

IT IS essential to remember that the information I provide is intended for educational and informational purposes only and should not be interpreted as personalised financial advice. For individualised financial advice, consult with a licensed financial advisor.

Here are some prompts to get you started when using GPT chat for personalised financial advice and guidance:

1. "I'm struggling with debt, what options do I have for getting out of debt?"
2. "How can I create a budget that works for my unique financial situation?"
3. "What retirement savings options are available to me, and which one is right for my financial goals?"
4. "I want to start investing, but I don't know where to begin. Can you help me understand the basics of investing?"
5. "Do I need life insurance, and if so, what type of life insurance is best for me?"
6. "I'm not sure what tax deductions or credits I'm eligible for. Can you help me understand the tax code better?"
7. "I want to create a comprehensive financial plan for my future. What are the steps involved, and where can I get started?"

16. Messaging during work

GPT Chat can provide guidance on how to use GPT chat efficiently for messaging during work. To communicate effectively through chat, it is crucial to keep the messages concise and professional to convey the intended message clearly. Here are some tips for using GPT chat for messaging during work:

- Use clear and concise language to communicate effectively. Keep messages short and avoid technical jargon or acronyms that may confuse the recipient.
- Use a professional tone in a work setting. Avoid using slang, emoticons, or overly casual language that may be interpreted as unprofessional.
- Ensure proper grammar and spelling. Proofread messages before sending them to avoid any errors that may impact the clarity of your message.
- Respond promptly to messages to avoid miscommunications or delays. Check your chat frequently and reply to messages as soon as possible.
- Ask for clarification if you receive a message that is unclear or confusing. Don't make assumptions as it may lead to miscommunication.
- Be mindful of sensitive information and use appropriate channels for such communication, such as encrypted messaging or secure email.
- Stay focused on the task at hand and avoid engaging in unrelated conversations or activities to increase productivity and avoid distractions.

USING GPT CHAT CAN BE an effective way of messaging during work, as long as one follows these guidelines to maintain professionalism, clear communication, and avoid miscommunications that may impact work performance.

HERE'S an example of how to apply these guidelines when using GPT chat for messaging during work:
Example:
Sarah needs to write an email to her boss, Mr. Smith, to request a

day off work. She's not sure how to phrase her request and wants to make sure her message is clear and professional. Sarah decides to use GPT chat to help her improve her message. She types in her draft message and receives feedback from the AI language model. The chatbot suggests she use a more formal greeting and add details about why she needs the day off. The chatbot also suggests she proofread her message for grammar and spelling errors before sending it. Sarah makes the recommended changes to her message and sends it to her boss.

In this example, Sarah effectively used GPT chat to improve her work message by receiving feedback and suggestions from the AI language model. She was able to refine her message, make it clearer and more professional, and increase her chances of getting her request approved.

17. Virtual language tutor: Use GPT chat to receive personalized language tutoring and practice.

Using a GPT chatbot as a virtual language tutor can be a great way to improve your language skills. To get started, you should first determine the language you want to learn and find a chatbot that supports language learning. Set specific language learning goals before starting the conversation, such as improving your listening comprehension, practicing your speaking skills, or learning new vocabulary. Once you have initiated the chat, try to practice regularly with the chatbot for a few minutes every day to build your confidence and improve your language skills over time. It's important to find a chatbot that provides feedback on your pronunciation, grammar, and vocabulary usage to help you identify areas where you need to improve.

If you want to improve your British English pronunciation, you can use a GPT chatbot that focuses on pronunciation practice. The chatbot will provide you with feedback on your pronunciation, help you identify areas where you need to improve, and give you practice exercises to help you improve your accent. With regular practice and feedback, you can make significant progress in your language learning journey.

. . .

EXAMPLE :

You: Hello, I'd like to improve my British English pronunciation. Can you help me with that?

GPT chatbot: Of course, I can help you with that. What specific aspect of your pronunciation would you like to work on?

You: I have difficulty pronouncing some words correctly. For example, I struggle with words that have silent letters.

GPT chatbot: Alright, let's start with some practice exercises. Here's a word for you to pronounce: "knight". Please try pronouncing it for me.

You: "nite"?

GPT chatbot: Very close! The correct pronunciation is actually "nait". Let's try another word: "debt".

You: "debt"?

GPT chatbot: Excellent! You pronounced that one correctly. Let's try another: "gnome".

You: "nome"?

GPT chatbot: Great effort! The correct pronunciation is "nohm". Keep practicing with words that have silent letters, and you'll improve your pronunciation over time.

You: Thank you for your help! Do you have any other tips for improving my British English pronunciation?

GPT chatbot: Sure! In addition to practicing words with silent letters, you can also try practicing common British English phrases and listening to British English speakers. You can also watch movies or TV shows with British accents to get more familiar with the language.

HERE ARE some prompts for the topic of using a GPT chatbot as a virtual language tutor for British/American English pronunciation:

1. What are some benefits of using a GPT chatbot to improve your British/American English pronunciation?
2. How can you use a GPT chatbot to practice specific sounds or words in British/American English?
3. What are some common pronunciation mistakes that non-

native speakers make in British/American English, and how can a GPT chatbot help address them?
4. What are some features to look for in a GPT chatbot designed to improve British/American English pronunciation?
5. Can a GPT chatbot replace a human language tutor for pronunciation practice, or are there limitations to using this technology for language learning?
6. How can you incorporate GPT chatbot practice into a broader language learning routine for improving British/American English pronunciation?
7. Are there any potential drawbacks or limitations to using a GPT chatbot for British/American English pronunciation practice, and how can you address them?

18. Build a CV and Cover letter with GPT chat

Here's how you can do it :

1. Begin by introducing yourself to the chatbot, and let it know that you want to create a CV and Cover letter.
2. Provide the chatbot with information about your educational background, work experience, and skills. This information will be used to create a customised CV.
3. Answer the chatbot's questions about your previous work experience, including job titles, company names, job duties, and accomplishments. Be sure to highlight your achievements and any relevant skills or certifications.
4. Provide the chatbot with your education history, including the name of your institution, degree(s) earned, and any relevant coursework or research projects.
5. Let the chatbot know what your career goals are and what type of job you're interested in pursuing. This will help it to tailor your CV to your specific needs.
6. Based on the information you've provided, the chatbot will generate a draft of your CV. Review it carefully, making any necessary changes or additions.

7. Once you're happy with your CV, the chatbot can help you create a customised cover letter. It will ask you questions about the job you're applying for and use that information to generate a cover letter tailored to the specific job and employer.
8. Review the cover letter and make any necessary changes or additions. Be sure to proofread both your CV and cover letter carefully before submitting them.
9. Once you're satisfied with your CV and cover letter, you can save them to your computer and use them to apply for jobs.

HERE ARE some prompts you can use to start a conversation with a GPT chatbot on building a CV and cover letter:

1. Can you help me create a professional CV and cover letter?
2. What information do I need to provide to create a personalised CV?
3. Can you guide me through the process of creating a cover letter?
4. How can I make my CV stand out from other applicants?
5. Can you provide tips for writing a successful cover letter?
6. What should I include in my CV if I have limited work experience?
7. How can I highlight my skills and accomplishments in my CV?
8. Can you suggest some action words to use in my CV and cover letter?
9. How long should my CV and cover letter be?
10. Can you review my CV and cover letter and provide feedback?

19. Generate a name for a podcast or webinar, or title for your book or article

Coming up with a name for your podcast or webinar, or a title for your book or article can be a difficult task. To generate a name or title, you should first identify the theme or topic of your content. Use descriptive words that capture the essence of the content, and consider using puns or wordplay to make it more interesting and engaging. You can use GPT chat to generate a list of potential names or titles based on the keywords or phrases related to your topic. Test your potential names or titles with a small group of people to get their feedback, and then narrow down your list to a few strong contenders. Choose the name or title that best fits your content and brand. Finally, do a quick online search to ensure that it's not already in use by another similar podcast, webinar, book, or article. Remember to choose a unique and memorable name or title that accurately reflects the content of your podcast, webinar, book, or article.

HERE ARE SOME RELATED PROMPTS:

1. Can you help me come up with a name for my podcast/webinar/book/article?
2. What are some tips for generating a catchy and memorable name?
3. How do I ensure that the name accurately reflects the content of my podcast/webinar/book/article?
4. Can you provide some examples of puns or wordplay that I can use in my name?
5. How can GPT chat help me generate a list of potential names or titles based on my topic?
6. What should I do if I can't decide between several strong contenders?
7. How do I know if a name or title is already in use by another similar podcast/webinar/book/article?
8. How important is it to have a unique and memorable name or title for my podcast/webinar/book/article?

9. Can you give me some ideas for names or titles based on a specific topic or theme?
10. How can I ensure that the name or title I choose will resonate with my audience?

20. Simplifies complex information

To simplify complex information using GPT chat, you should first identify the key concepts that you want to simplify and determine your target audience. Once you have these, use GPT chat to summarise the information in simple terms. Break down the information into smaller chunks, and use examples or analogies to help illustrate complex concepts. Avoid using technical jargon and instead use plain language. Finally, test your simplified information with a small group to ensure that it is clear and easy to understand. By following these steps, you can use GPT chat to make complex information more accessible to a wider audience.

LET'S say you are a teacher who needs to explain a complex scientific concept to your high school students. You are struggling to find a way to simplify the information without losing the important details.

You decide to use GPT chat to help you simplify the information. You enter the complex scientific concept into the chat and ask it to provide a brief summary in simple terms.

GPT chat responds with a summary that uses simpler language and breaks down the information into smaller, more manageable chunks. It also provides examples and analogies to help illustrate the concept.

You take the simplified information and present it to your students. You notice that they are able to understand the concept more easily and are more engaged in the lesson. You also receive positive feedback from your students, who appreciate the clear and concise explanation.

Overall, using GPT chat to simplify complex information has helped you better communicate the scientific concept to your students and improve their learning experience.

. . .

HERE ARE some prompts related to this topic:

1. Can you help me simplify a complex scientific concept for my high school students?
2. What are some tips for simplifying complex information without losing important details?
3. How can GPT chat help me break down complex information into smaller, more manageable chunks?
4. Can you give me an example of how GPT chat has helped simplify complex information in the past?
5. What are some ways to use examples or analogies to help illustrate complex concepts?
6. How can I ensure that the simplified information is still accurate and informative?
7. What are some common mistakes to avoid when simplifying complex information?
8. Can you recommend any resources or tools that can help me simplify complex information?
9. How can I test whether the simplified information is easy for my target audience to understand?
10. How important is it to simplify complex information, and what are the benefits of doing so?

16

How GPT Chat can help me at work?

GPT chat is a versatile tool that can be used in a wide range of work-related situations. Its ability to generate human-like text and provide information quickly can be beneficial for many different industries and professions.

One potential use case for GPT chat is in research and information gathering. Whether you need to find specific data or research a particular topic, GPT chat can quickly provide you with relevant information. For example, a journalist could use GPT chat to gather information on a breaking news story, or a healthcare professional could use it to research the latest medical findings.

Another potential use case for GPT chat is in writing and editing. GPT chat can help generate ideas, write drafts, and even proofread your work. This can be particularly useful for content marketers or bloggers who need to produce a large amount of high-quality content in a short amount of time.

GPT chat can also be useful in customer service, answering common customer questions and providing support. For example, an e-commerce business could use GPT chat to provide real-time customer support, allowing customers to get their questions answered quickly and efficiently.

Sales and marketing is another area where GPT chat can be useful.

By generating personalised marketing messages and analysing customer data, GPT chat can help businesses generate more leads and improve their sales strategies.

In training and development, GPT chat can be used to provide online training courses, answer employee questions, and track progress. This can be particularly useful for businesses with remote employees or those who need to provide ongoing training to staff.

Project management is another area where GPT chat can be used effectively. By helping to keep track of project milestones, deadlines, and team member responsibilities, GPT chat can help ensure that projects are completed on time and within budget.

Finally, GPT chat can facilitate communication and collaboration among team members, even if they are working remotely. This can help improve productivity and ensure that everyone is working towards the same goals.

Overall, the versatility of GPT chat makes it a valuable tool for a wide range of work-related situations. By using GPT chat effectively, businesses and professionals can save time, improve productivity, and provide better customer service.

17

Applications of GPT Chat

There are many potential applications of GPT chat, ranging from customer service and marketing to education and research. Here are some examples of how GPT chat can be used and how to implement them:

- Customer Service: GPT chat can be used to create automated chatbots that provide customer support 24/7. These chatbots can handle basic customer queries, such as order status, product information, and shipping details. To implement this, you can use a chatbot platform that integrates with GPT chat, such as Chatfuel, Dialogflow, or ManyChat.
- Marketing: GPT chat can be used to create conversational marketing campaigns that engage with potential customers and drive sales. For example, you can create a chatbot that asks questions about a customer's preferences and recommends products based on their responses. To implement this, you can use a marketing automation platform that integrates with GPT chat, such as Hubspot, Marketo, or Pardot.

- Education: GPT chat can be used to create interactive learning experiences for students. For example, you can create a chatbot that provides personalized feedback on students' writing assignments or quizzes. To implement this, you can use an online learning platform that integrates with GPT chat, such as Edmentum, Coursera, or Udacity.
- Research: GPT chat can be used to analyze large amounts of text data and extract insights. For example, you can use GPT chat to analyze customer reviews and feedback to identify common themes and areas for improvement. To implement this, you can use a text analytics platform that integrates with GPT chat, such as Lexalytics, MonkeyLearn, or RapidMiner.

TO USE GPT chat in these applications, you will need to have access to a GPT chat API or use an existing chatbot or conversational platform that integrates with GPT chat. You will also need to have a good understanding of natural language processing and machine learning to develop and train your chatbot or text analysis model. However, with the right tools and expertise, GPT chat can be a powerful tool for improving communication, engagement, and productivity in a variety of industries and applications.

HERE ARE some popular GPT chat applications and examples of how they can be used:

1. OpenAI GPT-3: This is one of the most advanced GPT chat models available and can be used for a wide range of applications, including customer service, content generation, and chatbots. For example, it can be used to create a chatbot that answers customer queries about a product or service, or to generate automated emails and social media posts.

1. Google's Dialogflow: This is a cloud-based platform for building conversational interfaces, including chatbots and voice assistants. It can be used for customer service, marketing, and education applications. For example, it can be used to create a chatbot that helps customers order food from a restaurant, or to create a voice assistant that provides guidance and support to students learning a new language.

1. Amazon Lex: This is an AI-powered chatbot platform that can be used to build voice and text-based conversational interfaces. It can be used for customer service, marketing, and education applications. For example, it can be used to create a chatbot that helps customers book travel arrangements, or to create a voice assistant that provides personalized tutoring to students.

1. IBM Watson Assistant: This is an AI-powered chatbot platform that can be used to build conversational interfaces for a variety of applications, including customer service, marketing, and education. For example, it can be used to create a chatbot that helps customers troubleshoot technical issues with a product, or to create a voice assistant that provides on-demand support to students learning a new skill.

APPLICATIONS OF GPT chat are varied and growing rapidly, with new use cases
    being developed all the time. Whether you are looking to streamline

your customer service operations, create engaging marketing campaigns, or provide personalized learning experiences to your students, there is likely a GPT chat solution that can help you achieve your goals.

18

How to create images using AI

Creating images using AI involves using machine learning algorithms to generate or manipulate digital images. The process usually involves training a neural network using a large dataset of images, which allows the AI to learn how to create or modify images based on patterns in the data.

There are several different techniques for creating images with AI, including:

1. Style transfer: This involves taking the style of one image and applying it to another image. The result is a new image that combines the content of one image with the style of another. This technique can be used to create unique and artistic images.
2. GANs (Generative Adversarial Networks): GANs are a type of neural network that consists of two parts: a generator and a discriminator. The generator creates new images, while the discriminator evaluates whether those images are real or fake. Over time, the generator becomes better at creating images that can fool the discriminator, resulting in high-quality images.
3. DeepDream: This is a technique that involves taking an

existing image and enhancing it using a neural network. The result is a surreal and dream-like image that highlights patterns and features in the original image.
4. Image recognition: AI can also be used to identify and classify objects within images. This can be useful for tasks such as automated image tagging or object detection.

PT chat is not specifically designed for creating images. While it is possible to use GPT-3 to generate text descriptions of images, the actual image creation would need to be done using other tools or software.

However, there are some tools that use GPT-3 to generate basic images based on user input. For example, DALL-E is a tool developed by OpenAI that uses GPT-3 to generate images from textual descriptions. Users can enter a description of an object or scene, and the tool will generate an image based on that description.

You can try Midjourney to create images from your prompts. Search some video on Youtube " create pictures with Midjourney" and you'll have a list of videos how you can do it just inserting a prompt for your image.

But it's so easy, just open Midjourney chatbot, and insert a prompt. And AI will generate a picture for you:

HERE'S a possible prompt example to create an image using AI:

"Generate a realistic landscape image of a beach at sunset. The image should have a warm colour palette with orange and pink hues. The beach should have smooth sand and gentle waves. There should be a few palm trees on the left side of the image and a small boat on the water in the distance. The sky should have a few scattered clouds with a gradient of colours from yellow to purple. The overall mood of the image should be peaceful and relaxing."

And you'll get a unique image, but you'll need a subscription to do this. So just think first if you need it.

Another option is to use online image generators that are designed to be easy to use, even for those without extensive design skills. These tools allow you to choose from a variety of templates and customize the images with your own text, colors, and graphics. Some examples include Canva, Crello, and Piktochart.

While these tools may not have the same level of complexity or customization options as professional design software, they can be a good starting point for creating basic images without the need for extensive design skills or knowledge.

Creating images using AI has the potential to revolutionize many industries, including art, design, advertising, and even medicine. As AI continues to advance, we can expect to see even more innovative applications of this technology in the field of image creation.

19

Future of AI

Artificial intelligence (AI) is a rapidly growing field with enormous potential to impact virtually every aspect of our lives. As AI technologies continue to evolve and mature, they are expected to transform many industries and sectors, driving innovation, productivity, and growth.

One area where AI is expected to have a significant impact is healthcare. AI-powered systems can help improve disease diagnosis and treatment by analysing large amounts of medical data, and it is also being used to develop personalised treatment plans based on a patient's unique genetic profile. In addition, AI can help automate administrative tasks in healthcare, freeing up medical professionals to focus on patient care. AI can also help with remote healthcare delivery, and improving healthcare access to the underserved population.

Another area where AI is expected to have a major impact is education. AI-powered systems can help provide personalised learning experiences that adapt to each student's unique needs and abilities, and can also help automate administrative tasks for teachers and school administrators. AI can help optimise the teaching process, improving the quality of education while reducing the workload of teachers.

AI is also being used in business to improve productivity and efficiency. For example, AI-powered systems can help automate routine tasks and provide data-driven insights that can inform decision-making. In addition, AI can help businesses optimise their operations and improve customer experiences. AI can also help improve supply chain management and logistics, enabling businesses to better manage their resources and reduce waste.

AI has the potential to address a range of environmental challenges as well, from climate change to natural resource management. For example, AI-powered systems can help monitor and predict environmental changes, and can also help identify areas where conservation efforts are most needed. AI can help with energy optimisation, waste management, and pollution control.

Finally, robotics is an area where AI is already having a major impact and is expected to continue to grow in importance. AI-powered robots are being used in manufacturing, healthcare, and other industries to perform a wide range of tasks, from assembly line work to surgical procedures. AI-powered robotics has the potential to improve productivity, reduce human error, and improve working conditions for human employees.

Of course, as AI technologies continue to advance, there are also potential risks associated with their use. These risks include job displacement, bias and ethical concerns, and privacy and security issues. However, many experts believe that these risks can be mitigated through careful planning and regulation.

The future of AI is likely to be complex and multifaceted, with both challenges and opportunities. However, there is no doubt that AI will play an increasingly important role in shaping the world around us in the years to come, and its potential to improve our lives and solve some of the world's biggest problems is enormous.

20

Future Directions for GPT Chat

GPT Chat is a rapidly advancing technology that has the potential to revolutionise the way we interact with digital devices. Looking towards the future, there are several exciting directions in which GPT Chat could develop.

Firstly, there is scope for improving the technology's language comprehension and context sensitivity. While GPT Chat is already capable of generating human-like responses to questions, it can sometimes struggle to understand the meaning behind words or to interpret the nuances of language. Future developments could therefore focus on enhancing its ability to comprehend language more accurately and respond in a more contextually appropriate manner.

Secondly, there is potential for increased personalisation and customisation of GPT Chat. Although it can already be customised to some extent, further advances could enable the technology to learn more about individual users and tailor its responses to their preferences and needs. This would help to enhance the user experience and make GPT Chat even more user-friendly.

Thirdly, there is potential for GPT Chat to be developed with enhanced emotional intelligence. While the technology is already impressive in its ability to generate human-like responses, it currently lacks the emotional intelligence of a human being. Further advancements could enable GPT Chat to better understand and respond to human emotions, which would be particularly useful in domains such as mental health care or counseling.

Fourthly, GPT Chat is already being used in a wide range of applications, from customer service to language translation to content creation. However, there are many more domains and applications where GPT Chat could be applied. For example, it could be used in fields such as law, finance, or education, where it could provide valuable insights and assistance.

Finally, it is important to consider the ethical and responsible use of GPT Chat. As with any AI technology, there are concerns about the potential risks and implications of using GPT Chat, and it is important to ensure that the technology is used in a way that is transparent, ethical, and beneficial to society.

Overall, the future directions for GPT Chat are promising, and there is great potential for this technology to continue to advance and improve. As AI becomes increasingly sophisticated, we can expect to see even more applications and uses for GPT Chat emerge, and for it to become an even more integral part of our daily lives.

21

Discussion of potential impact of GPT to society

GPT Chat is a rapidly developing technology that has the potential to revolutionise the way we communicate and interact with digital devices. Its ability to generate human-like responses to questions and understand the nuances of language makes it an exciting technology with far-reaching implications for society.

The Impact of GPT Chat on Employment:

One potential impact of GPT Chat on society is its effect on employment. As the technology becomes more advanced, it has the potential to replace human workers in certain industries, particularly those related to customer service and support. While this could lead to increased efficiency and cost savings for businesses, it also raises concerns about job loss and the need for retraining and upskilling for workers.

The Ethical Implications of GPT Chat:

Another important consideration is the ethical implications of GPT Chat. As with any AI technology, there are concerns about the potential risks and implications of using GPT Chat. For example, there are concerns about the use of GPT Chat for malicious purposes, such as creating fake news or spreading misinformation. It is important to ensure that the technology is used in a way that is transparent, ethical, and beneficial to society.

The Role of GPT Chat in Education:

GPT Chat also has the potential to transform education. It could be used to provide personalised learning experiences for students, tailoring its responses to their individual needs and learning styles. It could also be used to assist teachers in grading papers or providing feedback to students, freeing up their time to focus on other aspects of teaching.

The Impact of GPT Chat on Mental Health:

Another potential application of GPT Chat is in the field of mental health. It could be used as a tool to provide support and assistance to individuals struggling with mental health issues, providing a safe and confidential environment for individuals to discuss their feelings and concerns. However, there are concerns about the accuracy and reliability of GPT Chat in this context, and the need to ensure that users receive appropriate and effective support.

The Role of GPT Chat in Business:

GPT Chat has the potential to transform the way businesses interact with customers. It could be used to provide personalised customer support, answering questions and addressing concerns in real-time. It could also be used to analyse customer interactions and provide insights into customer needs and preferences.

The Impact of GPT Chat on Journalism:

GPT Chat has the potential to transform journalism by automating certain aspects of the news gathering and reporting process. It could be used to generate news articles or provide summaries of news stories, freeing up journalists to focus on investigative or in-depth reporting.

The Role of GPT Chat in Government:

GPT Chat could be used to improve the efficiency and effectiveness of government services, such as providing personalised assistance to citizens or analysing data to inform policy decisions. However, there are concerns about the potential for bias or errors in the technology, and the need for transparency and accountability in its use.

GPT Chat has the potential to have a significant impact on society, both positive and negative. It is important to carefully consider the potential implications of this technology and to ensure that it is used in a way that is transparent, ethical, and beneficial to society in various fields.

22

Conculsions

The field of natural language processing has seen a rapid growth in recent years, and the development of GPT chat by OpenAI has played a significant role in this advancement. GPT chat has become a powerful tool for generating human-like language and has opened up new avenues for applications in a variety of fields.

In this book, we have explored the development of GPT chat and its various applications, including language translation, content creation, customer service, and even mental health therapy. We have seen how GPT chat has the potential to revolutionise the way we interact with technology and how it can benefit businesses and individuals alike

Looking forward, it is clear that GPT chat will continue to play a significant role in the development of natural language processing and AI in general. As the technology becomes more sophisticated and more accessible, we can expect to see new and innovative applications of GPT chat that will continue to shape the way we interact with technology and each other.

In conclusion, the development of GPT chat represents a major milestone in the field of natural language processing and has already had a significant impact on a variety of industries. While there are still challenges and ethical considerations to be addressed, the potential benefits of GPT chat are immense, and we are excited to see where this technology will take us in the future.

Made in United States
Orlando, FL
16 July 2023